BEING AN ACTIVE CITIZEN
VOTING

by Vincent Alexander

Ideas for Parents and Teachers

Pogo Books let children practice reading informational text while introducing them to nonfiction features such as headings, labels, sidebars, maps, and diagrams, as well as a table of contents, glossary, and index.

Carefully leveled text with a strong photo match offers early fluent readers the support they need to succeed.

Before Reading

- "Walk" through the book and point out the various nonfiction features. Ask the student what purpose each feature serves.
- Look at the glossary together. Read and discuss the words.

Read the Book

- Have the child read the book independently.
- Invite him or her to list questions that arise from reading.

After Reading

- Discuss the child's questions. Talk about how he or she might find answers to those questions.
- Prompt the child to think more. Ask: Have you voted in a school election before? Did your choice win or lose? How did you feel about the outcome?

Pogo Books are published by Jump!
5357 Penn Avenue South
Minneapolis, MN 55419
www.jumplibrary.com

Copyright © 2019 Jump!
International copyright reserved in all countries. No part of this book may be reproduced in any form without written permission from the publisher.

Library of Congress Cataloging-in-Publication Data

Names: Alexander, Vincent, author.
Title: Voting : being an active citizen / by Vincent Alexander.
Description: Minneapolis, MN : Jump!, Inc., [2018] | Series: Being an active citizen | Includes bibliographical references and index.
Identifiers: LCCN 2018009880 (print)
LCCN 2018007469 (ebook)
ISBN 9781641280334 (ebook)
ISBN 9781641280310 (hardcover : alk. paper)
ISBN 9781641280327 (pbk.)
Subjects: LCSH: Voting—United States—Juvenile literature. | Elections—United States—Juvenile literature.
Classification: LCC JK1978 (print)
LCC JK1978 .A188 2019 (ebook)
DDC 324.60973—dc23
LC record available at https://lccn.loc.gov/2018009880

Editor: Kristine Spanier
Book Designer: Anna Peterson

Photo Credits: Blend Images - Hill Street Studios/Getty, cover, 1; ZUMA Press Inc/Alamy, 3; blue67 design/Shutterstock, 3 (vote art); Eti Swinford/Dreamstime, 4; Washington Post/Getty, 5; New York Daily News Archive/Getty, 6-7; Everett Historical/Shutterstock, 8-9; SuperStock/Getty, 10; filo/iStock, 11; Brand X Pictures/Getty, 12-13; AFP/Getty, 14-15; Robyn Mackenzie/Shutterstock, 16 (left); P Maxwell Photography/Shutterstock, 16 (right); Blend Images/Alamy, 17; Blend Images/Superstock, 18-19; Steve Debenport/iStock, 20-21; Jon Schulte/Shutterstock, 23.

Printed in the United States of America at Corporate Graphics in North Mankato, Minnesota.

TABLE OF CONTENTS

CHAPTER 1

THE RIGHT TO VOTE

The United States is a **democracy**. This means we **elect** our leaders. How? We vote.

What leaders do we elect?
Town council members.
Mayors. Governors. Judges.
Representatives. Senators.
We even vote for the president!

All **legal citizens** can vote. They must be at least 18 years old. But it hasn't always been this way.

In U.S. history, many people have had to fight for the right to vote. African Americans **protested** against unfair voting laws for 100 years.

Women also fought for the right to vote. In 1920, the Nineteenth **Amendment** passed. It said people could not be **denied** the right to vote because of their gender.

CHAPTER 2

VOTERS HAVE A VOICE

Voting is a **privilege**. In many countries, citizens cannot vote. Rulers make any decisions they want. They control the lives of the citizens. Our **founders** wrote the U.S. Constitution in 1787 to make sure this wouldn't happen here.

founders

We must make our voices heard.
One way is peaceful protesting.

Another way is to show up on election day. Voting is not a law. But it is a responsibility. It is how we make change in our towns, cities, states, and the country.

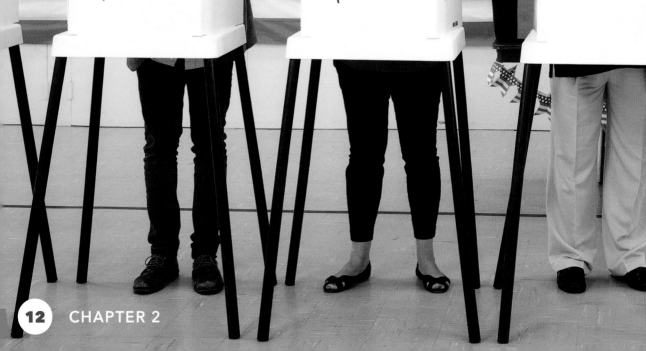

TAKE A LOOK!

A sample **ballot** can be found online before an election. You can use it to research **candidates**. You can even bring it with you to help you remember who to vote for. Take a look at this sample ballot.

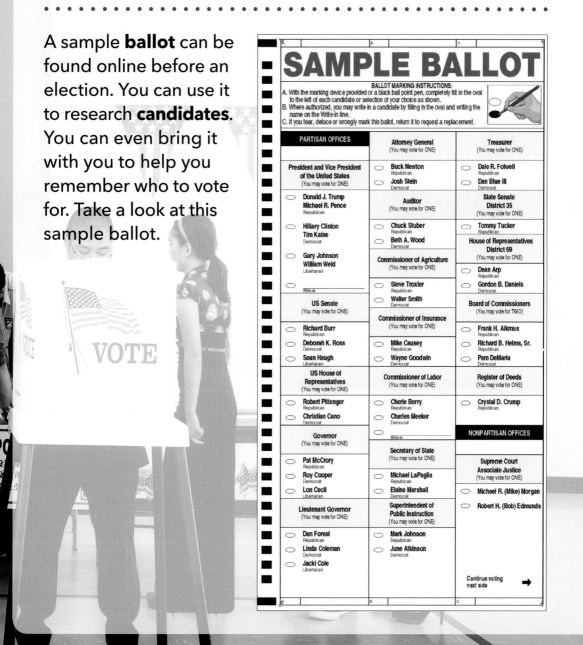

SAMPLE BALLOT

BALLOT MARKING INSTRUCTIONS:
A. With the marking device provided or a black ball point pen, completely fill in the oval to the left of each candidate or selection of your choice as shown.
B. Where authorized, you may write in a candidate by filling in the oval and writing the name on the Write-in line.
C. If you tear, deface or wrongly mark this ballot, return it to request a replacement.

PARTISAN OFFICES

President and Vice President of the United States
(You may vote for ONE)
- Donald J. Trump / Michael R. Pence — Republican
- Hillary Clinton / Tim Kaine — Democrat
- Gary Johnson / William Weld — Libertarian
- Write-in

US Senate
(You may vote for ONE)
- Richard Burr — Republican
- Deborah K. Ross — Democrat
- Sean Haugh — Libertarian

US House of Representatives
(You may vote for ONE)
- Robert Pittenger — Republican
- Christian Cano — Democrat

Governor
(You may vote for ONE)
- Pat McCrory — Republican
- Roy Cooper — Democrat
- Lon Cecil — Libertarian

Lieutenant Governor
(You may vote for ONE)
- Dan Forest — Republican
- Linda Coleman — Democrat
- Jacki Cole — Libertarian

Attorney General
(You may vote for ONE)
- Buck Newton — Republican
- Josh Stein — Democrat

Auditor
(You may vote for ONE)
- Chuck Stuber — Republican
- Beth A. Wood — Democrat

Commissioner of Agriculture
(You may vote for ONE)
- Steve Troxler — Republican
- Walter Smith — Democrat

Commissioner of Insurance
(You may vote for ONE)
- Mike Causey — Republican
- Wayne Goodwin — Democrat

Commissioner of Labor
(You may vote for ONE)
- Cherie Berry — Republican
- Charles Meeker — Democrat
- Write-in

Secretary of State
(You may vote for ONE)
- Michael LaPaglia — Republican
- Elaine Marshall — Democrat

Superintendent of Public Instruction
(You may vote for ONE)
- Mark Johnson — Republican
- June Atkinson — Democrat

Treasurer
(You may vote for ONE)
- Dale R. Folwell — Republican
- Dan Blue III — Democrat

State Senate District 35
(You may vote for ONE)
- Tommy Tucker

House of Representatives District 69
(You may vote for ONE)
- Dean Arp — Republican
- Gordon B. Daniels — Democrat

Board of Commissioners
(You may vote for TWO)
- Frank H. Aikmus — Republican
- Richard B. Helms, Sr. — Republican
- Pam DeMaria — Democrat

Register of Deeds
(You may vote for ONE)
- Crystal D. Crump — Republican

NONPARTISAN OFFICES

Supreme Court Associate Justice
(You may vote for ONE)
- Michael R. (Mike) Morgan
- Robert H. (Bob) Edmunds

Continue voting next side →

How do we know who to vote for? We study the candidates. How? By visiting their websites. Reading newspaper articles. Talking to friends and relatives. Watching **debates**.

What issues are important to you? Do you agree with what the candidates say about them?

WHAT DO YOU THINK?

What is something you would like to see changed where you live? Research your leaders. Are any of them working on it?

CHAPTER 3

ELECTION DAY

It is election day. Workers arrive at **polling places** early. They set up the rooms. They turn on computers. They stack ballots. Do they have enough pens? Everything must be ready when voters arrive.

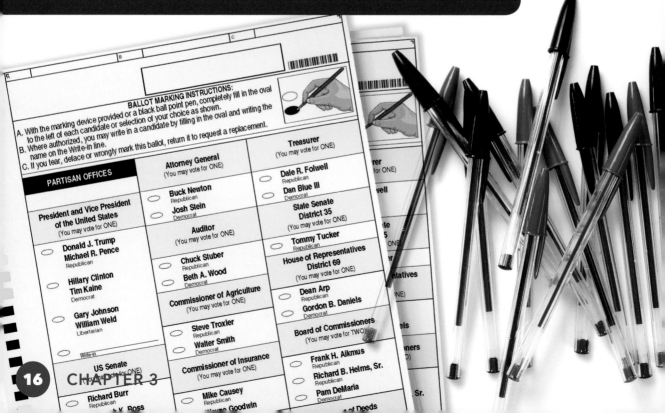

Voters line up. They check in. Is the voter a legal citizen? Is the voter at least 18? If yes, the voter gets a ballot.

booth

After receiving a ballot, a voter may enter a **booth**. Or sit at a table. Voting is private.

When the voter is done filling out the ballot it goes into a machine. The machine helps count the votes. The voter might take an "I Voted" sticker.

WHAT DO YOU THINK?

Have you gone to a polling place with an adult? Was it loud or quiet? What else did you notice?

At the end of the day, the votes are counted. They are added to votes from other areas. All votes are equal. The **majority** of votes wins. We have new leaders!

Making our voices heard through voting is an important duty of active citizens. It keeps our democracy working!

DID YOU KNOW?

We vote for the president once every four years. But elections take place every November. For who? Other leaders who run our towns, cities, states, and country. It is important to vote every year.

ACTIVITIES & TOOLS

TAKE ACTION!

RESEARCH A CANDIDATE

In Chapter 2 of this book, information about how to research a candidate is provided. Is an election coming up where you live? Research at least one candidate.

① In a notebook, list three topics the candidate mentions on a website or in a newspaper article.

② Next to each topic, write down what the candidate believes about those topics.

③ Now consider your own opinions. Do your beliefs match the beliefs of the candidate? Why or why not?

④ You may be too young to vote, but you can discuss the candidate's ideas with your parents or guardians. Let them know what you think. Encourage them to vote!

GLOSSARY

amendment: A change that is made to a law or legal document, such as the U.S. Constitution.

ballot: A document used to cast secret votes.

booth: A small, enclosed space where a voter can cast a ballot.

candidates: People who are running in an election.

debates: Discussions in which people express opinions.

democracy: A form of government in which the people choose their leaders in elections.

denied: To have been refused or not allowed to do something.

elect: To choose someone by voting for him or her.

founders: People who created the structure and first laws of the United States.

legal citizens: People who are born in the United States or have been given the rights of U.S. citizenship.

majority: More than half of the people in a group.

polling places: Places where votes are cast and recorded during an election.

privilege: A special right or advantage given to a person or a group of people.

protested: Made a demonstration or statement against something.

INDEX

TO LEARN MORE

Learning more is as easy as 1, 2, 3.

1) Go to www.factsurfer.com

2) Enter "voting" into the search box.

3) Click the "Surf" button to see a list of websites.

With factsurfer, finding more information is just a click away.